YOUNG PEOPLE'S STORY OF
OUR HERITAGE

YOUNG PEOPLE'S
STORY OF
OUR HERITAGE

FINE ART

by

V. M. HILLYER and E. G. HUEY

New Edition Designed and Revised by Childrens Press, Chicago

Consultants

*Ruth Esserman, Chairman, Art Department
Highland Park High School, Highland Park, Illinois*

*Everett Saunders, Art Lecturer, Northwestern University
Art Consultant, Wilmette School System, Wilmette, Illinois*

Meredith Press, New York

Illustrations in the order in which they appear

Contents

_____

Acknowledgments

Cover: Pablo Picasso, **A Mother Holding a Child and Four Studies of Her Right Hand,** detail, black crayon on cream paper
Courtesy of The Fogg Art Museum, Cambridge, Mass., Harvard University, Meta and Paul J. Sachs Collection

Georges Mathieu, **Homage to Richard I, Duke of Normandy**
Collection Richard Brown Baker, New York City. Transparency by Francis G. Mayer, New York City

Page 2: J.A.D. Ingres, **Stamaty Family, Group Portrait,** Louvre, Paris
Art Reference Bureau

Frontis: Jean Baptiste Camille Corot, **Church at Marissel,** Louvre, Paris
Art Reference Bureau

Opposite: Winslow Homer, **Flamborough Head, England,** detail, gouache and wash
Courtesy of The Art Institute of Chicago, Mr. and Mrs. Martin A. Ryerson Collection

———————————

Designed by John Hollis

Edited by Joan Downing

FINE ART

The Last Two Hundred Years

Stirring Times in France

It was the year 1793. The French Revolution had overthrown the government of the king of France. The common people had stood hardships and injustice until they could stand them no longer. Then they had rebelled. France had been made a republic. The heads of hundreds of people—enemies of the republic—were being cut off. The king and his family had been put in prison. It was voted that they too should lose their heads.

One of the men who voted yes to the question, "Shall the king be killed?" was Jacques Louis David (Dah-veed). David was a painter. He believed the revolution was right, even though he had been one of the court painters. By court painter we mean the king's own painter.

Jacques Louis David, **Napoleon at Mt. St. Bernard**
Chateau, Versailles

Eugène Delacroix,
The Lion Hunt

Some of the revolutionists had read about the old Roman republic. They liked to think of themselves as strong and brave like the ancient Romans. They liked to think of their republic as like the old Roman republic. So it became the fashion in the revolution to imitate the old Roman heroes. David got the actors in the theaters to wear Roman costumes instead of French clothes. Soon other people were trying to dress like the Romans. They even made their furniture in imitation of Roman furniture. David found that the people wanted Roman pictures, so he painted many pictures of scenes from Roman history.

Today we think that David's paintings are not so wonderful as the revolutionists thought them. But they are important because they set a style in painting. The old Roman and Greek days are known as the classical times, so this style that David made so popular is called the *classical* style of art. And David and the other classical style artists said that no other kind of painting was worth doing. They made many rules for painting that they expected all good artists to follow.

David had begun painting pictures of the Romans even before the revolution. One of these paintings is called *The Oath of the Horatii*. The Horatii were three brothers who were champion fighters. Rome was at war with another city. Instead of letting the two armies fight, which would have meant the death of many men, each side agreed to pick three fighters and let them fight it out to see which city should win the war. The Romans chose the three brothers, who took a solemn oath to win for Rome or die trying. David's picture shows them taking this oath.

When the fight was ended, two of the brothers had been killed. But the third one had managed to kill the other three fighters and so to win the war for Rome.

Another famous Roman picture by David shows the women stopping the fight between the Romans and the Sabines by running out between the two battle lines.

David was also a portrait painter. He painted a portrait of a French lady, Madame Récamier, who is shown lying on a couch. The couch is Roman in style and the lady's dress shows the Roman styles that French women wore then.

After the revolution came Napoleon. Napoleon made himself emperor of France. David admired Napoleon greatly and painted several pictures of him. He painted him on a rearing horse, crossing the Alps. He painted him being crowned emperor. (Napoleon crowned himself.)

But after Napoleon, there came another king—of the same family as the poor king who had lost his head. Naturally, David wasn't court painter to *him*—not after having voted for the other king's death! In fact, David had to run away from France, and he lived in Brussels for the rest of his life.

But the strict rules of the classical style of art lived on. David had had many pupils and some of them became famous painters, too. One of these pupils was the artist Ingres (Angr). Ingres was a wonderful draftsman. That means that the lines he drew were beautifully done. He thought more about the lines in a picture than the color or the light. All classical painters tried to make the lines and shapes in their pictures more important than the colors. Their colors are dull and lifeless. Ingres is probably best known for his portraits. And the portraits that he drew in pencil and did not paint at all show how great a draftsman he was (see page two).

Baron Gros (Grow) was another pupil of David, and it was too bad that he was, for the classical pictures he painted, as much as possible following David's strict rules, were not so successful as those he painted in another style. Gros kept trying to paint great classical pictures and was brokenhearted when he found he couldn't do them well. His really fine pictures he thought little of, because they were not about Greeks and Romans. These others are interesting to us because they pictured the events that were taking place then.

Napoleon thought it would be a good idea to have a painter with his army. So he made Gros Inspector of Reviews in the army so that the painter could go with the troops and paint the battles. Gros watched the fighting himself, so he did not paint war as a glorious thing. He showed the heroism of the soldiers, but he showed their terrible suffering too.

Now we come to a French painter who did not believe at all in classical painting. The strict rules that the classical painters said all artists should follow made this artist angry. He was Delacroix (Della-crwah). Delacroix led a revolt against the classical style of painting. Painters who thought as Delacroix did were called *romanticists*. The romanticists didn't see any sense in painting Greeks and Romans. They wanted to paint what was going on in the world at that time. The romanticists revolted against the classical style in another way. They believed in color. They thought color was more important than beautiful line drawing.

Of course the classical painters hated the romanticists and tried to do all they could to stop them. But Delacroix and his followers became more and more popular and finally they took the place that the classical artists had once held.

Delacroix painted pictures of the Crusaders, of Bible stories, of the people of Algiers, and of the war going on in his time between the Greeks and the Turks.

One of Delacroix's paintings is called *Liberty Leading the People*. It is supposed to show a scene in a new French Revolution that took place in 1830 when there was fighting between the people and the soldiers of the king in the streets of Paris. It is a stirring picture, full of action and movement. It has really a double meaning. The classical style of painting that tried to keep all other ways of painting out of France needed to be overthrown too. And this picture may be thought of as Liberty leading romantic art against the too-strict rules of classical art.

Eugène Delacroix, **Orphan at the Cemetery,** Louvre, Paris

The First Great English Painters

Do you know what an international picture show is? It is a group of pictures brought together from different countries so that people can see how much alike and how different the paintings are.

Let's suppose all the great countries in Europe had decided to have an international picture show in 1700 A.D. We shall have to call it a make-believe show because the various countries never thought of such a thing in those days.

We'll say it's 1700. Each country can send only one picture and the best will get a prize.

Now let's say that all the pictures have arrived:

A Titian from Venice

A Michelangelo from Rome

A Velasquez from Spain

A Rubens from Flanders

A Rembrandt from the Netherlands

A Dürer from Germany

A Poussin from France

But where is England's picture? Every important country except England has sent a famous painting. Now, England is one of the greatest countries in this year 1700, but all we get from England is a letter saying that she is very sorry but she can't send us a picture by a famous English artist because she hasn't had any famous artists. What? One of the greatest countries in Europe—perhaps the greatest—has no painters?

But though England had had no famous painters by 1700, she soon made up for lost time. Her first famous artist was three years old in 1700. His name was Hogarth. And after

---

William Hogarth, **The Shrimp Girl,** National Gallery, London

Hogarth came many more artists. If we had held our make-believe international picture show in 1800, England would have had plenty of paintings to choose from.

Hogarth began as an engraver of silver. Then he learned to engrave on copper and make prints from his copper plates. These prints were very popular and he sold enough of them to make a good living. But all the time he wanted to be a painter. So he painted pictures, but he was so well known as a print maker that very few people considered him a great painter. They preferred his prints and engravings. He found that he could make engravings of his paintings and sell prints much more readily than the paintings themselves.

Probably all boys and girls like to read the funny papers. A newspaper comic strip is usually very poorly drawn. You could hardly call it art. And yet Hogarth, in some of his paintings, used the same idea as the funny papers. He used to make a series of six or eight pictures about the same people, showing what happened to them from time to time. Only instead of being simply funny, Hogarth's pictures were meant to show how bad certain things were in England at that time. They were often humorous, as well. That kind of humor we call *satire*.

Hogarth printed one series of pictures about a man who was trying to be elected to Parliament. One picture shows the man making a speech. Another shows him hiring men with clubs to make the people vote for him, another shows him bribing voters—that is, paying them to vote for him. Each of the pictures is a good painting by itself, but the whole series was supposed to be seen together, like the different pictures in a comic strip. And these pictures made a great impression on the Englishmen of Hogarth's time. Perhaps they did help make things better as Hogarth hoped they would. Today elections are certainly run as fairly in England as anywhere in the world.

Hogarth painted portraits too. He painted a portrait of himself with his little dog. He painted a picture of *The Shrimp Girl*. In London in Hogarth's time people bought shrimps from girls who carried the shrimps around in a basket on their heads.

Hogarth caught the shrimp girl's smile as Hals caught the smiles in the portraits he painted—with quick, sure strokes of the brush. If you put this painting side by side with Dürer's portrait of his father, it looks unfinished. And yet it tells you as much about the real shrimp girl as Dürer's picture tells you about his father.

About the middle of the eighteenth century, while Hogarth was still painting, two other Englishmen were rising to fame as great painters. One was Sir Joshua Reynolds, the other Thomas Gainsborough. Both were best known as portrait painters. Sir Joshua Reynolds was a few years older than Thomas Gainsborough, so I'll tell you about him first.

I'll begin this story with an African pirate. The pirate was a kind of Arab king who was holding up ships in the Mediterranean. The British were sending a captain with a squadron of ships to talk things over with the pirate.

This captain was a friend of Reynolds and invited him to come along on his warship. Reynolds accepted the invitation and when he got to Italy he stayed there, to study the great paintings of Michelangelo, Titian, Correggio, and Raphael. He liked Michelangelo best. He liked Michelangelo so much he became deaf! That sounds strange, but it is true. Reynolds was working in the Sistine Chapel, studying Michelangelo's paintings. He was sitting in a draft, but was so interested in the pictures he didn't even notice the draft. Not till he got up to go did he notice that anything was wrong. But after that he began to grow deaf, and soon he had to use an ear trumpet.

Reynolds went back to London and became the favorite portrait painter of the city. There were no cameras in those days, so no one could have a photograph taken. Instead, people went to an artist and had their portraits painted. Poor people could not afford portraits by so expensive a painter as Reynolds, so most of his portraits are of lords and ladies and their children. The king knighted him, and he became Sir Joshua Reynolds.

Sir Joshua worked hard and tried to make every picture he painted better than the one before. He was especially good at painting women and children. Have you ever heard of pictures called *The Strawberry Girl, Master Hare, The Age of Innocence*, and *Mrs. Siddons as the Tragic Muse?* These are some of Reynolds's best known portraits.

Sir Joshua Reynolds, **Master Hare,** Louvre, Paris

25

Unfortunately, Reynolds was always trying out new kinds of paints and oils, so that many of his pictures have become faded or cracked. Some even faded soon after he painted them. But this didn't make him less popular. A friend of his said, "A faded portrait by Reynolds is better than a fresh one by anybody else."

The other portrait painter, Thomas Gainsborough, liked best to paint landscapes. He couldn't sell the landscapes, however, and so he continued to paint portraits all his life. And very fine paintings they are. He made the people he painted look so graceful and charming that he was in great demand. Gainsborough's colors are not so rich and glowing as Reynolds'—they are more silvery and gray.

One of Gainsborough's paintings that has become world famous as *The Blue Boy* is thought to have been painted

---

Thomas Gainsborough, **Lady Walking in St. James Park,** chalk
British Museum, London

because Reynolds had said a picture with much blue in it could not be beautiful. So Gainsborough painted *The Blue Boy* to prove Reynolds was wrong. Gainsborough didn't seem to like Reynolds for some reason, and was always as rude to him as could be. Perhaps he was jealous of the other painter. But before Gainsborough died he asked Reynolds to forgive his rudeness and told him how much he admired him and his work.

Gainsborough painted portraits of many of the same people that Reynolds did. They both, for example, painted the Duchess of Devonshire and Mrs. Siddons. Which of the portraits of these two ladies is better it would be hard to say.

Gainsborough's landscapes are more admired than they were when he was alive. Though they are not so well-known as his portraits, they will help us to think of him as an excellent British painter.

opposite left: Sir Joshua Reynolds,
Mrs. Siddons as the Tragic Muse

---

opposite right: Thomas Gainsborough, **Mrs. Siddons**
National Gallery, London

Three Englishmen
Who Were Different

Ghosts! Do you like ghost stories? Stories of haunted houses, of chains clanking at midnight, of misty white shapes that you can see right through? Of course the best time to read a ghost story is at night. Then, though you know the story can't be true, it makes you feel creepy.

But I'll tell you of one ghost that won't make you feel creepy. This ghost won't even make you tremble in your boots. It's the ghost of a flea. It makes one smile just to think of the ghost of a flea, coming back to haunt, perhaps, the dog who scratched him to death. This flea ghost isn't in a ghost story. He's a more unusual ghost than that, for this ghost had his portrait drawn by a celebrated artist.

The artist who drew the picture of *The Ghost of a Flea* was William Blake. He was an Englishman who was living in London at the time the American colonies were fighting their Revolutionary War.

William Blake was very different from any artist I've told you about so far. For one thing, besides being an artist, he was a poet. For another thing, William Blake's pictures are not at all like the pictures of any other artist. For still another thing, William Blake saw visions. A vision is something like a dream—it is a sight a person sees only in his mind. Some people say that Blake was a little crazy, just a *little* crazy. Perhaps he was only different.

William Blake, **The Morning Stars**, from the "Book of Job," engraving, 1825, British Museum, London

Blake had always wanted to be an artist. He studied engraving for many years, until he became an expert engraver. And then, when he set up in business for himself, he engraved his poems and his pictures together on one plate. This was a new idea that he himself invented. Before then the pictures in a book were engraved on a metal plate, but the words of the book were printed with a printing press. Blake made both pictures and words on the same plate, so the story was really part of the pictures and the pictures were part of the story.

He made and engraved pictures not only for his own poems but for many other books also. The most famous of all his pictures are the ones he made to illustrate the Book of Job in the Bible. These pictures of Job and his troubles are hard to forget, once you have seen them.

Most of Blake's pictures that you see in books look like drawings. That is because they are made up of lines. An engraving has to be made with lines. But Blake usually made a painting for each picture before he engraved it, and these paintings show he could use colors as well as lines.

Blake had had new ideas about painting and soon there were other English artists who had new ideas. But before telling you about them I'll ask you a question.

Have you ever seen a tree in summertime that had brown leaves? A live tree, I mean. Anyone would know that a live tree has green leaves. Yet if you saw a picture of a tree painted about the time of Blake you would be surprised to see that it had brown leaves. As I told you, Gainsborough is noted for his landscapes. Perhaps you won't think him so great a painter when you learn that the leaves of his trees were usually painted brown. Now, those landscape painters must have known that real trees are green, but still they kept painting them brown. Strange, is it not? They must have thought the brown leaves looked better in their pictures.

But after Gainsborough came an English painter named John Constable and after him there were no longer so many brown trees. Constable tried to give his picture the colors he saw in real landscapes. This sounds easier to do than it really is. Even the whitest white a painter can put in a picture isn't nearly as bright as a dull sky on a rainy day. And if the picture sky *can't* be as bright as the real sky is, all the other colors have to be made a little darker than the real colors, to make the sky look bright enough. For the darker the dark parts of a picture are, the brighter the bright parts will look next to them.

Being darker doesn't keep the picture from being beautiful, but it does keep it from looking exactly like the real landscape. So if a way could be found to make the colors in a painting look brighter, then artists could make an outdoor picture look more really outdoorsy. And that is what Constable did. He found a way of making paints look brighter. Instead of putting the paint on smoothly, he put it on in little dabs of thick color so that if you touch one of his paintings with your finger it feels rough.

Constable found that when he used little dabs or spots of color, the whole picture became brighter. The old way of painting a green field, for instance, was to paint it all green. Constable's way was to paint the field with separate little spots of green and yellow and blue. And, strange to say, these make the field look all green, unless you get too close to the picture. When you do get too close you can see the separate spots, but at a little distance the whole field becomes one color—a brighter green than if it had been painted a smooth, solid color in the first place.

_____

John Constable, **Wivenhoe Park, Essex**

National Gallery of Art, Washington, D.C., Widener Collection

John Constable,
The Hay Wain,
National Gallery,
London

Joseph Mallord William Turner, **The Lake From Petworth House,** National Gallery, London

So we remember Constable for two helpful improvements in landscape painting. He made trees green instead of brown. He made pictures brighter by using rough little spots of paint in place of smooth, solid colors.

Many people believe the best English painter of all was the landscape painter Turner—Joseph Mallord William Turner. He came nearer than any other painter to catching the brightness of color and light of nature. He loved to paint the sea and the sun.

Now, of course the sun itself is so much brighter than any paint that no one can ever put it in a picture and expect it to look like the real dazzling, brilliant sun. But a painter can paint something that people can see is meant to be the sun. Turner often did something that Claude Lorrain had sometimes done. He painted "into the sun." That is, he painted a scene with the sun right ahead. Usually he put the sun behind a cloud or in a mist or at sunset so that its brightness would not look too unlike the brightness of the real sun.

We know very well that no painter can find bright enough colors for a sunset, but people who saw Turner's sunset pictures said they were too bright to be true. They aren't true, but not because they are too bright, as these people said. It is because they aren't bright enough.

Turner could also paint the sea better than any one before him. He was a painter of seascapes as well as landscapes. Before he painted the sea he really *studied* it—how it looked when it was calm and how it looked in a storm—how it looked in the rain and in sunshine. Once he had himself lashed tight to the mast of a ship in a storm so he could study the sea without being washed overboard.

One of Turner's most famous paintings is called *The Fighting Téméraire* because that was the name of the old warship in the picture. The *Téméraire* had become too old for further use and the picture shows her being towed, by a puffing tug, to the dock—to be broken up. It is just sunset and the water of the harbor reflects the gorgeous orange and yellow of the sky. It is the end of the day and the end of usefulness for the old ship that had served her country for many years.

Joseph Mallord William Turner, **Grand Canal, Venice**

The Metropolitan Museum of Art, Bequest of Cornelius Vanderbilt, 1899

41

The Poor Barbizon Painters

———————

Why should I tell you about very poor painters? If a painter can't paint good pictures, why mention him at all? Because . . . these poor painters in this chapter *did* paint good pictures. They were poor in money, not poor in painting.

One of these poor, good painters was a Frenchman named Corot (Ko-rō). He was poor because no one would buy his paintings. Not until he was fifty years old did he sell a single picture. He wasn't quite as poor as that sounds, however, because his father gave him an allowance of so much a year. It was a very small allowance, but Corot managed to get along on it.

After Corot finished school he wanted to be a painter. But his father was in the linen business, and into the linen business the son had to go. Still he kept hoping he could be a painter, and finally his father let him stop selling linen and begin to study painting. Corot went to Italy for several years and became a landscape painter. Then he went back to France. He painted many fine landscapes, but no one seemed to want to buy them.

Now, at this time some other painters who were very poor in money found they could live more cheaply in the little village of Barbizon than they could in the city of Paris. And they found, too, that the country around Barbizon was a much better place in which to paint landscapes. There they could see the forests and streams and fields that they loved to paint. So these poor-in-money painters moved to little cottages in and near Barbizon. We call them the Barbizon Painters.

It was Corot's idea to live in Barbizon. He liked to get up early in the morning and go out to study the trees and fields in the early light of dawn, when often the dew was on the

Jean Baptiste Camille Corot, **Just Before Sunrise**

ground and everything looked misty. He would make sketches, or quick drawings, of what he saw, and then come home and paint. He liked twilight and moonlight, too, and often painted twilight and moonlight landscapes. His pictures have a magical, dreamy beauty that has made them famous all over the world.

When he was an old man Corot's pictures began to sell. Money and fame came rolling in at last. Corot had always loved to help other people in any way he could, and now that he was wealthy he had a fine time giving most of his money away to people who needed it.

Corot was always cheery and happy with his friends, although his landscapes often seem dreamy and sad instead of cheerful and gay. Everyone loved him and called him Father Corot. It is nice to know that he finally became famous.

Another Barbizon painter was much poorer in money than Corot. He was one of the first to go to Barbizon. He took his wife and children and lived in a little three-room house that had no wooden floors, just packed earth. Yet he was one of the greatest painters of France, Jean François Millet (Mee-lay).

Millet had always been poor. His father was a farmer, or peasant, and when Millet was a boy he worked on his father's farm. When he saw some pictures in an old Bible, he started to draw. At the rest hour in the fields the other workers would all take naps, but young Millet would spend the time drawing pictures. Finally the people in the village where he lived gave him a little money to go to Paris to study art.

When Millet got to Paris he had a terrible time. He was awfully shy and not used to city ways, so he didn't get along well at all. He barely made enough money for food by selling little pictures he painted. He liked best to paint the poor farmer people or peasants whose life he knew so well, and at last when he was almost starving someone bought one of his peasant paintings. This gave him enough money to get out of Paris and go to Barbizon, and in Barbizon he lived the rest of his life.

Millet's pictures of peasants at work were painted in an unusual way. The painter would go out on the farms and watch the people at work—digging, hoeing, spreading manure, sawing wood, churning butter, washing clothes, or sowing grain. Then he would come home and paint what he had seen. His memory was so good that he could paint at home without a model and get all the movements of his figures right. When he did need a model he would ask his wife to pose for him.

One of Millet's paintings is called *The Sower*. It shows a man planting seed. Have you ever seen a farmer sowing a field? Today it is so often done with horses and a machine, that perhaps you don't know what a swing there is to it when it is done on foot. The sower's hand keeps time with his step. It reaches into his bag for seed and then swings backward to scatter the seed, and with each swing of his hand the sower strides forward. In Millet's picture the sower has been working hard, but his swinging step and outflung arm still move smoothly, in time, like a machine. Only the man's head shows how tired he is.

Millet made several pictures of *The Sower*, all somewhat alike. The most famous *Sower* is now in the United States.

Another picture that is as famous as *The Sower* is called *The Gleaners*. A gleaner is someone who picks up what is left in

the field after the wheat has been harvested. When farmers are very poor, as they were near Barbizon, even the little that the gleaners can find is a help.

Many copies have been printed of still another picture by Millet. This famous painting is called *The Angelus*. It shows a French farmer and his wife stopping their work in the fields to bow their heads as they hear the church bell ring out the call to prayer, the Angelus.

Like Corot, Millet at last was recognized as a great painter before he died. But he always remained poor, and when he died his friend Corot had to give his widow money to live on.

Some of the other Barbizon painters became famous too. They all used to meet and talk in a big barn where they had tacked drawings on the walls.

Jean Francois Millet, **The Gleaners,** Louvre, Paris

opposite: Jean François Millet, **Self-Portrait**

Claude Monet
**Old St. Lazare
Station, Paris**

Claude Monet,
**Rouen Cathedral,
West Façade, Sunlight**

Claude Monet,
The River

Impressionism

Let's suppose you are blindfolded. I'm going to guide you, blindfolded as you are, out to a field this morning. I'm going to stand you so you are facing a haystack and then I'm going to take the handkerchief off your eyes and let you look at the haystack for five minutes. Then I'll blindfold you again and lead you back. It's a strange game, isn't it?

Let's play it once more. The first time when you looked at the haystack it was ten o'clock in the morning. This time I'll let you look at the same haystack for five minutes about five o'clock in the afternoon. And this time the haystack will look quite different from the way it looked at ten. It's the same shape, but the colors and light and shadows are all so different that the five o'clock haystack makes a picture to your eye very different from the ten o'clock haystack. Every little while during the day the haystack changes in color and brightness. That's why I let you look at it for only five minutes at a time— so the light would not change and give your eye another picture.

Now, I'm sure you can see that if an artist painted a picture of the haystack for every hour of the day he would have many pictures of the same haystack, but each picture would be different from all the others.

That is just what some French artists did not so many years ago. Then they gave an exhibition of their work. They hung their paintings on the walls of a room so that people could come and see them. The people who came found these paintings were very different from any they had ever seen before. The pictures were like your quick view of the haystack. They showed the colors and light that the artists had seen in quick views of the things they were painting. These views were called impressions. And so the painters soon got the name of *impressionists*.

Earlier painters never thought of doing such a thing. They painted a horse one color and a haystack another, no matter whether the light always made them *look* that color or not. Really a black horse or a yellow haystack is not always black or yellow. The color depends on the light. The light shining on a black horse may make him look blue in places. But you know so well that a horse *isn't* blue that you don't notice how blue he really may look in certain lights!

Painters always used to paint shadows brown or gray or black. But if you look carefully at a real shadow it is often not brown or gray or black at all. It's just as apt to be green or blue or purple or some other color.

Of course bright light and color on an object outside was always hard to paint, because paints are not nearly so bright as light. But if you remember what I told you about the painter Constable, you will see how these impressionist artists made their colors look bright and like sunlight. They put the colors on in little dots and dashes. Putting colors on in dots and dashes of separate colors really does make them look brighter. They almost seem to shimmer like real sunlight. But it also makes the pictures look quite different from the older kind of painting.

For this reason the people who saw the French exhibition of the impressionists weren't very much pleased. These people had been used to one kind of painting, and the change was so great that they couldn't like the new kind nearly as well at first.

But after a while the impressionists came to be understood better. People saw that they were trying out a new way of painting and that what they were doing might be very worthwhile. One of the impressionists, named Claude Monet (Monay), used to go out with a carriage full of canvases and spend all day painting the same scene. He used a different canvas each time the light changed the color and appearance of the thing he was painting.

For instance, Monet painted fifteen pictures of the same haystacks and in each one had a different color and light effect. He painted twenty pictures of the front of a French cathedral as it was seen at different times of day, and each picture was different. They make an interesting series, but when you see one of these pictures by itself you are apt to be a little disappointed because the forms, or the shapes, in the painting are not so important as you think they should be. Monet was interested in the light and color, not especially in the form or shape.

Another Impressionist had a name much like Monet. His name was Manet (Man-ay). In fact, Manet was the painter who really started the impressionists. Manet didn't break his pictures up into so many little glittering spots as Monet did.

Edouard Manet,
The Fifer
Louvre, Paris

Indeed, it was only in the last ten years of his life that Manet used that kind of painting very much. Someone asked Manet once who the chief person was in one of his impressionist pictures.

"The most important person in any picture," Manet answered, "is the light." And that was what the impressionists tried to show in their paintings.

opposite: Edouard Manet, **Le Journal Illustré**

Postimpressionism

Postimpressionism means the same as *after* impressionism, which means the newer kinds of painting that came after the impressionistic paintings. You remember that Monet's work is impressionism, where light is "the most important person."

The father of postimpressionism was Paul Cézanne (Say-zann). He was a Frenchman, like Manet and Monet. At first he was an impressionist himself, but he said he wanted to make impressionism something solid and lasting like the art of the old masters. And after a while his work did become more solid, although none of his pictures became as well known as those of the old masters. Cézanne worked hard all his life at painting, but he never became popular as a painter until after his death. Luckily for him, he had money enough to live on without having to sell his paintings, for he found he couldn't sell them —no one wanted to buy them.

upper right: Paul Cézanne, **Self-Portrait,**
Berner Kunstmuseum, Berne

lower right: Paul Cézanne, **The Card Players**

The Metropolitan Museum of Art, Bequest of Stephen C. Clark, 1960

Vincent van Gogh,
Self-Portrait

Vincent van Gogh,
Bedroom at Arles

Another postimpressionist who was younger than Cézanne had a very different kind of life. This other painter didn't live quietly on a farm in southern France as Cézanne did, as you will soon see. His name was Vincent Van Gogh (pronounced Van Goch, the Goch rhyming with the Scotch word *loch*). He was a Dutchman. He tried working in an art store for his living, but if he thought his customers wanted to buy poor pictures, he gave them such lectures that he didn't get along well at all. So he tried being a schoolmaster for a few months. I don't believe he could have been a very good teacher, because he had a violent temper. Then he decided to be a clergyman— a minister. This didn't work, either, because he soon got tired of the college for ministers where he was studying. And so he set out as a missionary to the workers in the Belgian mines. He felt so sorry for these poor miners that he gave away all his money and he himself nearly starved.

His brother sent him money to live on and persuaded him to go to Paris to study art. Then Van Gogh went to live in a little town in southern France, and there he painted many pictures.

These paintings are made up of squirming lines of paint instead of the dots of paint that the impressionists used. A friend of his said, "He paints so fiercely that it is terrible to watch him." His pictures look as if he had painted them with fierce intensity.

And now comes a sadder part of Van Gogh's life. His mind began to give way. He began to go crazy. One day a friend of his who was a waitress in a café where Van Gogh sometimes went, asked him for a present and just in fun she said to him, "Well, if you can't give me anything else, you might give me one of your big ears."

Just before Christmas the waitress received a package. She thought it was a Christmas present. But when she opened it, out fell—an ear! The waitress was horrified. Poor Van Gogh was found in bed, completely out of his mind. He had cut off his right ear with a razor.

Of course he had to be taken to an asylum, where he finally got well enough to paint some more pictures. But the attacks of brain trouble kept coming back and during one of them Van Gogh shot himself.

A third postimpressionist was named Paul Gauguin (Go-ganh). Gauguin was a Frenchman of a different kind from Cézanne, and he led a life almost as strange as Van Gogh's.

Gauguin began a different life early. He ran away from home when still a boy, got on a ship and went to sea. He made several voyages as a sailor to different parts of the world. Then he came back to Paris and went into business.

Perhaps Gauguin would never have become a painter if he had not run away to sea. For one day when he was walking down the street he came to a shop window that had some paintings in it. These paintings had the brightness and color that Gauguin had seen in the faraway Pacific isles. They brought back to him memories of his voyages so clearly that he asked who the painters were. Thus he became acquainted with the postimpressionists who had painted these pictures. Gauguin began then to paint too. He became a friend of Van Gogh and even lived with that artist for a while before Van Gogh lost his reason. Later, Gauguin moved to another part of France.

But he could not forget the beautiful tropic islands of the Pacific he had seen on his voyages. One day he packed up again and sailed for the island of Tahiti. There in Tahiti the painter found the life he liked best. He lived like one of the native islanders and there he painted best pictures.

These paintings are bright with the color of the tropics and show in their brightness the people of the islands in their play and rest and work. These South Sea pictures are the ones that made Gauguin a famous painter.

upper right: Paul Gauguin, **Tahitian Woman with Children**

lower right: Paul Gauguin, **The Burao Tree (Te Burao)**

Early American Artists

Now we come to painting in America. I'll have to tell you right at the beginning that there is much more American painting, and that there are many more American artists, than I have room to tell you about in this book. America has had artists since before the American Revolution and today there are as

above: Gilbert Stuart,
**Athenaeum Portrait of
George Washington**

left: Gilbert Stuart, **The Skater**

opposite: Benjamin West,
Penn's Treaty with the Indians

Independence National Historical Park, Philadelphia

above: Charles Willson Peale,
John Paul Jones

right: John Singleton Copley,
Portrait of Paul Revere

Courtesy, Museum of Fine Arts, Boston

many good painters at work in America as in any country in the world—perhaps more.

The first American artist to become really famous was Benjamin West. Benjamin West's family lived in Pennsylvania when the woods were still full of Indians. There he was born and there he grew up. As his family were Quakers, the Indians were friendly to them, for the Quakers had made a treaty with the Indians to buy their land from them instead of just taking it by force or by cheating.

When Benjamin West was a boy he loved to draw pictures. The Indians were pleased when he drew pictures of them. Of course he didn't have any paints or paint brushes nor even any pictures to look at. There weren't such things in the little frontier village where he lived. So the boy was delighted one day when the Indians gave him some of the yellow and red paint that they used to paint their faces with. Benjamin ran home and showed the paints to his mother. Then his mother gave him some bluing which she used in washing clothes. Now he had yellow, red and blue paint, but no paint brushes. How do you think he got a brush? He used the cat!

Yes, he cut some hairs off the cat's tail and made them into a paint brush. When the first brush wore out, he got some more hairs from the cat. After a while the poor cat had hardly any hair left on her tail and was beginning to look very ragged!

When Benjamin West grew up he went to live in Philadelphia, and there he worked hard to become a good painter. Then he decided to go to Europe where he could see and study famous paintings. When he reached Rome he was taken to see a statue of a Greek god called the Apollo Belvedere.

"It looks like a Mohawk warrior," he said, thinking of the strong and graceful Indian braves of Pennsylvania.

West then went to England and settled in London. He became a very popular painter. The king, George III, liked him and his work so much that he made him court painter. And Benjamin West never returned to America. But he always welcomed American artists who came to London and was very generous and helpful to them. In fact, his studio was a kind of school for young men learning to paint, and many well-known American painters studied there. He was like a father to them all.

West's pictures often were very large and usually were filled with many figures, though he did paint some smaller portraits.

They were admired by everyone and some people even said they promised to be as great as the paintings of Michelangelo. These days we think West's paintings are not really very great paintings, but isn't it pleasant to hear of an artist's pictures being well thought of while he was alive and could enjoy their success? Many painters have had to struggle all their days as nobodies, their pictures not admired until after they died. So it's nice that the opposite happened to *this* painter.

One of West's best-known paintings is *The Death of General Wolfe*. General Wolfe was leader of the British soldiers when they fought the French at Quebec to decide whether France or England should own Canada. The British won, but General Wolfe was shot. Both the French and English were helped by Indian warriors. There is an Indian in the picture. Because West grew up with Indians he could paint them even in England with the nearest Indian three thousand miles away.

The picture caused a great stir in London, because the soldiers in it are dressed in their regular uniforms. In England it was thought that all pictures of history should show people dressed as Greeks or Romans. Even the king told West he shouldn't put his figures in such modern costumes. But when the picture was finished everyone, including the king, said

West was right. After that, artists painted their figures in the clothes the people they painted really wore.

One of the young Americans who studied under West in London was Gilbert Stuart. He was born and raised in New England before the Revolution. He thought he could do better in old England, so he traveled to London. There he became a painter of really fine portraits. People then thought Benjamin West a much better painter than we now think he was, but Gilbert Stuart's paintings are just as well thought of today as they were when he painted them.

After living many years in England, Gilbert Stuart went back to America. It was now the United States of America, for the American Revolution had been fought and won. Stuart had come back, he said, to paint the portrait of George Washington, whom he greatly admired.

Washington posed for three portraits by Gilbert Stuart. The last of these three is the most famous and best-loved picture of Washington there is. It is called the Athenaeum portrait because it belongs to the Athenaeum Club in Boston. You can see a small copy of it on many United States postage stamps.

You may wonder why this portrait seems unfinished. The reason is that Gilbert Stuart liked it so well that he wanted to keep it. He had promised the portrait to Washington when it was finished, but it was never finished. The artist couldn't bear to finish it! Instead of the original, Washington agreed to take a copy that Stuart made of it for him. As a matter of fact the artist painted about fifty copies of the portrait from time to time and sold a copy whenever he needed money.

Gilbert Stuart went to live in Boston and never returned to England. He painted five other Presidents besides Washington and so is sometimes called the Painter of Presidents.

Now, there were, of course, other American painters in the early days of the United States. Most of them were portrait painters, because so many people wanted portraits. There were still no cameras to take photographs. It is from the portraits of these early painters that we know what the famous Americans and beautiful women of those days looked like.

These early portraits have become very valuable, so that many of them are now in museums. Some, however, still belong to the families whose ancestors had their portraits painted. When you look at a portrait by Copley, Sully, Malbone, Trumbull, or one of the Peales be sure to look at it carefully and with respect, for it is the work of one of the famous early painters of America.

John Trumbull, **Capture of the Hessians at Trenton**

More American Artists

You've probably heard of Robert Fulton, the inventor of the steamboat. But have you ever heard of Robert Fulton the painter? Does it seem strange they should have the same name? Then this ought to seem even stranger—they were born the same year. Stranger yet—they died the same year. But—

It's really not strange at all, because the painter and the inventor were the same Robert Fulton. Robert Fulton's first profession was portrait painting. He studied under Benjamin West in London.

I know you've heard of Samuel F. B. Morse, the inventor of the telegraph. But have you ever heard of Samuel F. B. Morse the painter? Does it seem strange they should have the same name? It's really not strange at all, because the painter and the inventor were the same Samuel F. B. Morse. Morse's first profession was portrait painting. He too studied under Benjamin West in London.

Both were inventors. Both were painters. Both were helped by West. And they weren't bad painters, either. Of course they weren't nearly such good portrait painters as Holbein or Hals or Dürer. But you'll find them in almost any history of American art.

I wish I could tell you more about these and the many other early American portrait painters. About Raphaelle Peale, or his brother Rembrandt, who first provided a city in the United States with gas lights for its streets (and also studied under Benjamin West). Or about their father, Charles Willson Peale, or John Trumbull, who also studied under West.

But I'll have to tell you instead about the next group of American painters. These were landscape painters. First came these interesting portrait painters, then came landscape painters.

Most of the early American landscape painters are not quite so well-known as the portrait painters. These landscape painters tried to put into their pictures all the little details that they saw in nature. Every stick and stone and bush was painted in very carefully, and their pictures as a whole weren't as good as they might have been if the painters had left out the little things so you could look at the whole picture at once. Instead your eye sees the picture piece by piece.

―――――――――――――――

Raphaelle Peale, **Still Life with Cake**

They usually painted scenes that were very impressive, like views of mountains and big rivers and valleys seen from hilltops. Finally, however, one landscape painter changed this. He painted everyday peaceful scenes, like a meadow or some trees. He left out the unimportant details so you could see a beautiful picture instead of just a copy of a piece of real country.

I don't mean you to think that the real country isn't beautiful. A real outdoor scene *is* beautiful—more beautiful, usually, than any picture of it could be. But, you see, a painter can never make his picture look exactly like the real, beautiful scenery itself and so it's often better for him to make his

---

George Inness, **June, 1882**

painting a beautiful thing and not try to make it exactly like a real scene. A painter has to do this mostly by trying to make you *feel* what he felt when he saw the scene, rather than trying to show you every little thing he *saw*.

So this painter of everyday peaceful scenes, whose name was George Inness, tried to make people *feel* how beautiful he thought the scene was. George Inness used very beautiful colors that harmonized, or went well together. If there were some bits of color in the real scene that would not harmonize with the other colors in the picture, he left them out. If the picture looks better without having every detail clearly put in, why not paint it without the detail? This is what George Inness

---

George Inness, **Etretat, Normandy**

Courtesy of The Art Institute of Chicago, Edward B. Butler Collection

Courtesy of The Art Institute of Chicago, Mr. and Mrs. Martin A. Ryerson Collection thought. So his landscapes gradually became better and better pictures as he learned to leave out the things he saw that would prevent the picture from being beautiful. George Inness was one of the best American landscape painters.

A painter very different from George Inness was Winslow Homer. Winslow Homer is famous as a painter of the sea. Its hard to help liking his pictures. Winslow Homer didn't care to paint quiet seas. He preferred stormy ones. His pictures of waves dashing high against the rocky New England coast have

_____

Winslow Homer, **The Herring Net**

been called the best sea paintings that any artist has done. Winslow Homer loved the sea. He built his house on the rocky coast of Maine, where he could always watch the ocean.

He loved to hunt and fish, too, and often went into the Adirondack mountains—they were really wild in those days—and there he painted hunting scenes and canoes shooting the rapids and the guides at work.

When Winslow Homer took a trip on the ocean south toward Bermuda or the West Indies, he painted sea scenes of stormy weather there. He was fond of painting the fishermen who went in their schooners to fish on the Grand Banks out at sea.

Winslow Homer, **Eight Bells**

Two European Americans

Paintings sometimes go visiting. In 1932 a famous painting was carefully taken from its home in the Louvre in Paris, put on an ocean liner, and allowed to go on a visit to New York. The last time this painting had been in the United States was fifty years before. Then, no one thought enough of it to pay the thousand dollars that its painter was asking for it. On its second visit crowds of people went to see the painting, and if anyone had offered many, many thousands of dollars for it he could not have bought it. For it is now one of the art treasures of the great French art museum and it is not for sale. In New York it was treated as an honored guest.

The man who painted this visiting picture named it *An Arrangement in Gray and Black*. But it became too well loved to be called by such an uninteresting name. So everyone calls it now simply *Whistler's Mother*. Whistler was the artist who painted it.

James McNeill Whistler was an American, but most of his life was spent in Europe. He was a very conceited little man. He quarreled with his friends and seemed to like making enemies wherever he went. This probably helped him to become famous, because it kept people talking about him. He was always news. Perhaps that is why he wore a monocle, which is an eyeglass for just one eye, and why he carried an extra-long cane and signed his pictures with a butterfly. He liked to be talked about. He liked to be news.

But of course, no matter how much people talked about him, Whistler would not have been a great artist if he had not painted good pictures. And every one agrees that his *Mother* is a good picture. It is a different kind of portrait from those artists had painted before. That is why it wasn't admired as much at first as it is now. Whistler's mother is shown sitting beside a wall. On the wall hangs a picture in a black frame. You can see that nearly everything in the painting is in straight lines except the old lady herself.

How big would you guess the portrait of Whistler's mother is? Would you be surprised to hear that the mother in the picture is life-sized? As she is life-sized, you can see that the painting is a rather large one.

Some of the colors in Whistler's paintings are surprising. Some of his pictures are almost all blue in color—dark blues and light blues and medium blues, all blended to make a picture that is unlike the picture of any artist who used many different colors. Some are almost all white. *The White Girl*, for instance, shows a girl in a white dress seen against a white background. You can guess that that is not the easiest kind of picture to paint and that Whistler must have been very skillful to do it successfully.

James Abbott McNeill Whistler, **Portrait of the Artist's Mother**
Louvre, Paris

Agraci—Art Reference Bureau

Courtesy of The Art Institute of Chicago, Potter Palmer Collection

Another famous American painter who lived in Europe most of the time was John Singer Sargent. During his lifetime Sargent became the most famous living painter of portraits. He painted portraits of many rich people and many important people. Indeed, it was an honor to have Sargent paint your portrait.

Most of Sargent's portraits are no doubt very good. They are still admired very much, but his wall paintings in Boston are some of the best things he did. When the Boston Public Library was built, Sargent was asked to decorate the walls on the third floor. He painted religious pictures for these walls. One wall shows the children of Israel worshiping the old false gods. Underneath this is a long row of Hebrew prophets from the Old Testament. These prophets seem to be bewailing the evils of their people's ways.

On another wall Sargent painted saints and angels, with the crucified Christ in the center. He painted these figures with bands of real gold about their heads and with the figure of Christ carved like a statue as well as painted. People who saw them marveled that a portrait painter could paint these large wall decorations so splendidly. Now visitors to Boston go to the library just to admire the wall paintings there.

James Abbott McNeill Whistler, **Gray and Green, The Silver Sea**

John Singer Sargent, **Robert Louis Stevenson**

John Singer Sargent, **Daughters of Edward D. Boit**

Remington and Bellows

Do you like pictures of the wild West? Pictures of the Indians with their horses and dogs and rolled-up tepees taking the trail to new hunting grounds? Pictures of cowboys with their six-shooters and lariats, riding the herd or roping broncos? Pictures of hunters with their fur caps and trusty rifles, making their way through a heavy snowstorm? Pictures of soldiers of the United States cavalry patrolling the Indian country to keep order and protect property?

There was an American artist who painted such pictures very well. His name was Frederic Remington. Frederic Remington didn't sit home in a studio and ask Indians to come and pose for him. He went out to the wild West and painted them as he saw them living their daily lives. Even if Frederic

Remington had never written books about his life in the cowboy country, we should know by his paintings that he had lived there among real cowboys and Indians.

At first Remington didn't paint. He drew. For when he began to make pictures he was an illustrator. His job was to draw pictures in black and white for magazines and books. He was something like a human camera, trained to put down on paper, with pen and ink, life in the West just as it was, so people in the East could know what it was like.

Often illustrators do not become great painters, and at first Remington wasn't a great painter. When he began to paint with colors instead of simply drawing with pen or pencil, he showed the cowboys and Indians all right, but the colors he used were too bright and glaring. Of course on the plains and badlands of the West the colors that he saw were really bright and glaring in the brilliant sunlight and clear atmosphere. Gradually, however, his pictures became better paintings as he learned to use the bright colors better. His later pictures are really fine paintings, I think, and not just brightly colored illustrations.

Frederic Remington didn't paint the exciting happenings only. He liked to paint his Indians, for instance, as plain everyday Indian people and not to have them always dressed in feathers and warpaint. In other words, his pictures show us the real Indians, lazy or hard working, bad or good, dirty or clean, out hunting or at home on the reservation; and not just the picture book kind of Indians which you can see in a wild West show or in the movies. His soldiers are not always dressed up for parade or marching forth to a stirring band, like picture book soldiers, but are real men, cooking their suppers over the campfire, guarding wagon trains, cleaning their horses. His cowboys are real cowboys working for their living, not just the sort of cowboys we see in the movies. "Men with the bark on" is what Remington called these rough and ready men of the West.

And as for horses! Frederic Remington, let me tell you, could paint horses that were *real* horses. People aren't all alike. Neither are horses. Frederic Remington's horses aren't just picture book horses any more than his Indians are picture book Indians. Each horse is a special horse, different from any other horse. They are stupid or bright, wicked or gentle, lazy or full of life, just as real horses are.

Besides being a wonderful illustrator, a writer, and a good painter, Remington was a sculptor. He made statues of men on horseback that seem full of life and action.

So, if you want to see what the real wild West was like, not so many years ago, find a book illustrated by Frederic Remington. You'll really enjoy the pictures.

Frederic Remington, **The Howl of the Weather**

Courtesy of the Remington Art Memorial, Ogdensburg, New York

Remington was an American painter who painted American people. So was a later painter named George Bellows. George Bellows also painted the kind of pictures I think you'll like, only *his* pictures are of the eastern part of the country, especially in and about New York city. Bellows was such a good baseball player on his college team that he almost became a professional ball player, but decided to be a painter instead. He always liked athletics.

Some of his pictures show men and boys swimming along the New York waterfront, some are of polo games and some very well-known ones are of boxing matches. George Bellows painted other pictures of quieter subjects. He painted some fine pictures of old ladies and little girls.

He was an illustrator, too, as Remington was, but Bellows's illustrations were made in a very different way. They were made first on smooth stone and then printed with ink on paper from the stone. This kind of picture is known as a lithograph. Bellows was an unusually fine lithographer. During World War I Bellows made a famous lithograph showing the English Red Cross nurse, Edith Cavell, who was shot by the enemy as a spy.

George Wesley Bellows, **Dempsey and Firpo**

Courtesy of The Art Institute of Chicago, Friends of American Art Collection
Yale University Art Gallery, New Haven

One of Bellows' well-known paintings is of the boxing match between Dempsey and Firpo for the heavyweight championship of the world. Firpo was a South American boxer who was very strong. He was called the Wild Bull of the Pampas because of his tremendous strength. Once in the match the Wild Bull knocked Dempsey right through the ropes and down into the laps of the people looking on. But this didn't seem to damage Dempsey much, for he finally won the match. Bellows' picture shows Dempsey sailing out of the ring after Firpo's powerful punch. The picture is very dark in some places and very bright in others, because all the light was turned on the ring like a big ceiling spotlight on the stage. The picture shows how well Bellows could paint furious action.

Bellows also could paint a quiet picture. The portrait of his mother isn't very much like Whistler's picture of his mother, yet the two mothers seem to be about the same age. Notice the dark and light in his picture of his mother. Bellows liked to have some very dark parts and some very light parts in his paintings, and also in his lithographs.

It would be fun to tell you of the artists who are still alive and painting pictures while you are growing up. I have hardly mentioned the wall paintings—murals we call them—that are being used more and more to decorate the rooms in new buildings in America. You remember those of Sargent in the Boston Public Library.

Almost every large city in the United States now has good mural paintings in some of its buildings. If you live in a city, try to find out where these mural paintings are and then go to see them. They are very interesting. When you learn the name of the artist who painted them, see how much you can learn about his other paintings and about him.

opposite left: George Wesley Bellows, **My Mother**

---

opposite right: George Wesley Bellows, **Lady Jean**

Modern Art

Why, a six-year-old child could paint a better picture than that!" said the man.

"At least it has plenty of bright colors," said the woman. "Look at all that yellow and orange. I like it. Perhaps it's supposed to be a sunset."

"It looks more like a fried egg to me," the man said.

The man and woman were in an art museum. They were standing before a painting that really didn't look much like either a sunset or a fried egg. It was all made of yellow and orange paints except for a small dark blue square near one corner. As they moved on to the next painting, the man shook his head. "Modern art is too much for me," he said. "I just don't understand it."

Many people are puzzled by paintings that are not pictures of objects. Such paintings are called *nonobjective* paintings. Nonobjective paintings are not supposed to look like sunsets or fried eggs or people or houses or any other objects.

Have you ever tried to find pictures of objects in the clouds? Did you ever see a cloud that looked like a lion? Many times one can see clouds that look like a landscape with hills and valleys and harbors and islands. But seeing objects in the clouds doesn't make the clouds more beautiful. The clouds are beautiful whether or not we can use our imagination to see pictures in them.

Nonobjective paintings can be beautiful also. They don't have to look like some object that we can recognize. Sometimes you can enjoy them more if you don't puzzle your head over what objects they are supposed to look like. Just remember they are not supposed to look like anything—except a non-objective painting.

Artists who paint nonobjective paintings sometimes say, "A camera can make a picture of an object. A photograph will look like the real object. It will have realism. Why should a painter always try to make a picture look realistic? Why should a painter try to do something that a photographer can do with a click of the camera's shutter?"

Of course, most artists still paint pictures of objects. All modern paintings aren't nonobjective.

opposite above: Hans Hofmann, **The Golden Wall**

---

opposite center right: Jackson Pollock, **Grayed Rainbow**

---

opposite lower left: Pablo Picasso, **Head of the Acrobat's Wife (Woman with Helmet of Hair)**

Courtesy of The Art Institute of Chicago,
Mr. and Mrs. Frank G. Logan purchase prize fund

Courtesy of The Art Institute of Chicago, Gift of Kate L. Brewster

Courtesy of The Art Institute of Chicago, Gift of the Society for
Contemporary American Art

above:
Pablo Picasso,
The Three Musicians

below:
Pablo Picasso,
Le Gourmet

opposite:
Wassily Kandinsky
**Improvisation with
Green Center (No. 176)**

Courtesy of The Art Institute of Chicago, Arthur Jerome Eddy Memorial Collection

There are many modern paintings of objects, however, that are just as puzzling to some people as nonobjective paintings. That's because some people think a painting should show objects just the way they look to your eye or to a camera. They think the objects in these paintings should look real—that they should be realistic.

But a painter may not want to paint objects realistically. He may want to get into the picture some of the feeling he himself has about the object. He may want to use his imagination about the object.

Perhaps the artist may want to show all four sides of the object in the same picture. Usually when you look at an object you don't see more than two sides. When you look at a table, for instance, you know it has four legs but often you can see only two legs at once.

One of the best-known of modern painters at first painted pictures that showed people and objects as they really looked. They were realistic paintings. Then he got tired of painting realistic pictures. He tried other ways of showing objects. Some of his paintings, for example, show the front view and side view of a person's face in the same picture.

This painter's name is Pablo Picasso. Picasso was born in Spain but most of his work was done in France.

Look at the pictures by Picasso in this chapter. Two of them are realistic paintings. See how differently the other one is painted. It is not realistic at all. You could never mistake this picture for a photograph of three musicians. The three musicians are there in the picture all right but you can see they are not painted realistically.

Which picture do you like better? Do you think the nonrealistic picture is more interesting than the other one?

Would you say *The Three Musicians* is a nonobjective picture? It isn't, because it shows objects—the musicians. We can simply call it a nonrealistic picture.

Another way of painting is called surrealism. In a dream anything can happen. In a surrealistic painting anything can happen too. People can have heads made of cabbages. People

Salvador Dali, **Mae West**

111

can have bodies made of bureau drawers or have trees growing out of their ears, just as in a dream.

One famous surrealistic painting shows several watches. They look exactly like real watches except for one thing—they bend. They are limp, like pancakes. There are ants in one of the watches. Why should ants be in a watch? There doesn't have to be a reason, because the painting is surrealistic.

This painting was made by a man named Salvador Dali, who was born in Spain but left there to live in the United States.

Dali is the best-known of the surrealistic painters. Most of their paintings are clearly and smoothly painted with great skill. They are realistic paintings except that the objects in the pictures are often impossible objects. If there *were* limp watches, however, that's the way they would look.

Surrealistic paintings are puzzling just as a dream is puzzling. They are interesting and fun to look at just as a dream is fun—unless it's a nightmare. Often the artists who paint surrealistic pictures make them still more puzzling by giving them strange titles. The title of the limp watches is *The Persistence of Memory*. What does that mean? Your guess is probably as good as anyone's.

When you next visit an art museum see how many non-objective, nonrealistic, and surrealistic paintings you can pick out.

More Modern Painters

_____

If you were an artist you might think it more fun to paint a picture than to go to the circus. Artists like the circus but they also love to paint. That's why they are artists.

An artist named John Steuart Curry loved to paint pictures. Painting was his business. He also loved the circus. The circus was his hobby. So, for a while, he combined the two. He joined the circus and traveled with it so he could paint pictures of it. He painted pictures of the acrobats, trapeze performers, elephants, and equestriennes.

John Steuart Curry was born in Kansas. Besides circus pictures he painted many pictures of Kansas, especially of farm life in Kansas. One of his pictures shows a tornado in Kansas. Many people have never seen a tornado, but in parts of Kansas tornadoes happen so often that people build storm cellars where they can go to be safe from these powerful whirlwinds. The foreground of Curry's tornado painting shows a farmer and his family hurrying into their storm cellar. It's an exciting picture. Will the tornado hit the farmhouse and tear it to pieces? Will the family be safe? Will their barns be destroyed? Will the tornado ruin their crops?

John Steuart Curry's pictures are modern paintings, but they are not at all like the modern art that you read about in the last chapter. Modern art includes many kinds of paintings. Painters keep trying new ways of painting and it's a good thing they do. If artists always painted the way artists painted in the past their paintings would get tiresome. Nonobjective and nonrealistic paintings were new ways of painting when they were started. But they aren't the only kinds of modern art. In this chapter all the paintings are modern but you can tell easily that they are not like nonobjective, or nonrealistic, or surrealistic paintings.

John Steuart Curry, **The Tornado**

Thomas Hart Benton, **Aaron**

Grant Wood, **American Gothic**

Edward Hopper,
Early Sunday Morning

Edward Hopper, **Nighthawks**

The Tornado is a modern painting of a modern scene. *The Midnight Ride of Paul Revere* by Grant Wood is a modern painting of a scene in the past. This picture has the same title as the famous poem by Longfellow. It shows Paul Revere galloping on his horse through a New England village to warn the people that the redcoats are coming. Bright moonlight makes it easy to see the village church, the houses, the trees, the road, and the swiftly moving horse and rider. Lights are being lit in the houses Paul Revere has passed. Minutemen carrying muskets will soon be marching from the village to the battle that began the war of independence.

Not all of Grant Wood's paintings are of exciting events. One very famous painting he called *American Gothic*. It shows an elderly Iowa farmer and his wife looking straight out from the picture. Behind them is a wooden house with the Gothic-style

---

Andrew Wyeth, **Young America**

trimmings that some American houses still have. The man and woman look like serious, honest, kindly, hardworking people. Grant Wood's home was in Iowa and he liked to paint pictures of his own state.

Both Grant Wood and John Steuart Curry were from the great middle western part of the United States. A third famous painter from central United States is Thomas Hart Benton. He painted pictures of his native state of Missouri. Many of his paintings are large murals on the walls of public buildings. One of these large paintings is called *Huck Finn and Jim*. Mark Twain's book *Huckleberry Finn* tells of Huck's trip down the Mississippi on a raft with his friend Jim, who was escaping from slavery. The picture shows them on their raft.

Edward Hopper is another modern painter. His pictures are mostly of the eastern part of the United States. *Nighthawks*, however, might be a scene in any large city during the early morning hours when nearly everyone has gone home except the few who sit in this restaurant for one last cup of coffee. It is an unusual subject for a painting. Scenes like this don't often inspire a painter by their beauty. But Hopper has caught the loneliness of the quiet hours in the nearly deserted city. Notice the contrast between the darkness of the night outside and the glow of the lights inside the restaurant.

One of the differences between many modern artists and artists of the past is that artists now so often paint common, everyday subjects—people and places that are familiar to all of us. In Renaissance times and for long afterward most of the subjects chosen by painters were important people—kings and queens, lords and ladies; or they were gods and goddesses, or religious subjects, or beautiful scenery. Very seldom did the ordinary, unimportant people and scenes get painted. A few painters like the Breughels in Flanders, Hogarth in England, Millet in France, and Vermeer in Holland did paint the people that most artists found uninteresting. But now most artists paint people and scenes that are part of the familiar life of their countries.

Edward Hopper also painted *Ground Swell* which is just as different as can be from *Nighthawks*. Instead of a dark scene in a huge city, it is a picture of waves and sunshine and the outdoor fun of sailing a boat.

Andrew Wyeth is another modern American artist who paints in the realistic tradition.

Do you know any artists? There are hundreds of painters in America today. You have more chance of knowing an artist now than ever before in history. Certainly more people are painting now than ever before. The paintings of Curry, Wood, Benton, and Hopper are merely samples of hundreds that could have been chosen for this chapter. Many people are painting just for the fun of it. Painting isn't their chief job. They just like to paint. For example, Winston Churchill, the great prime minister of Great Britain during World War II, took up painting as a hobby and became very good at it.

One country that hasn't been mentioned in this book is Mexico. Between World War I and World War II Mexican artists became known all over the world for their paintings. The most famous Mexican artist is Diego Rivera. He painted many of his pictures on the walls of buildings. Most of these murals are in Mexican buildings but some are on walls in the United States. He liked to paint pictures of working people and especially of the Mexican Indian workers.

In the picture called *Man and Machinery* the whole painting is filled with people and machinery. This painting is on a wall in Detroit.

In the last two chapters you have learned several things. Modern paintings are of many kinds. Some of these are called nonobjective, and nonrealistic, and surrealistic. Many others are realistic. Many new ways of painting are being tried out. There are more artists than ever before. The United States has many good painters. So has Mexico.

Nearly all countries in the world now have good painters. So, wherever you go, you should be able to find paintings worth looking at carefully.

upper right: Diego Rivera, **Madame Marcoussis**

lower right: Diego Rivera, **North Wall: Part Production and Assembly of Motor,** detail

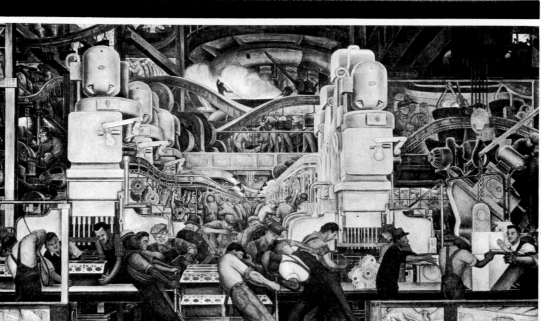

INDEX: *Young People's Story of Fine Art, The Last Two Hundred Years*